A Sum of Destructions

poems by

Theodore Weiss

■

1994

Louisiana State University Press
Baton Rouge and London

Copyright © 1986, 1987, 1988, 1989, 1990, 1991, 1992, 1994 by Theodore Weiss
All rights reserved
Manufactured in the United States of America
First printing
03   02   01   00   99   98   97   96   95   94   5   4   3   2   1

Designer: Glynnis Phoebe
Typeface: text, Bembo/display, Copperplate Gothic B-C
Typesetter: G & S Typesetters, Inc.
Printer and binder: Thomson-Shore, Inc.

Library of Congress Cataloging-in-Publication Data
Weiss, Theodore Russell, 1916–
    A sum of destructions : poems / by Theodore Weiss.
        p.   cm.
    ISBN 0-8071-1932-6. — ISBN 0-8071-1933-4 (pbk.)
    I. Title.
    PS3545.E4735S86   1994
    811'.54—dc20   94-11179
                                                                        CIP

Poems in this volume, usually in earlier versions, first appeared in the following publications:
American Poetry Review: "Fractions," "Later than Lately," "One Not One," "A Private Life,"
"Shorthand," "Flypaper," "Through Our Hands"; *Beloit Poetry Journal:* "A Crust"; *Green Mountain
Review:* "A Poem" (now "The Moths"); *New Criterion:* "A Parisian Air," "Something Kept"; *New
Republic:* "Bad Times\Mother" (now "Bad Times"); *Paris Review:* "A Foreign Tongue" (now
"Tongue-Tied"); *Partisan Review:* "A Matter of Degree"; *Pivot:* "A Place to Visit"; *Ploughshares:*
"When All the Walls Are Down" (now "The Garden Beyond"); *Poetry:* "An Old Cart,"
"Satisfied"; *Princeton Library Chronicles:* "Encore"; *Southern California Anthology:* "A Catch" (now
"The Net"); *Southern Review:* "A Troubled Glow," "Odds & Ends" (now "Deconstructed"), "The
Answer"; *Southwest Review:* "A Summer Drive"; *Triquarterly:* "Haunts," "Out of the Cold,"
"There," "The Future of the Past"; *Without Halos:* "Fractions." The author wishes to express his
gratitude to the editors of these publications. "A Sum of Destructions" first appeared in Weiss, *The
Catch* (New York, 1951).

Publication of this book has been supported by a grant from the National Endowment for the Arts
in Washington, D.C., a federal agency.

The paper in this book meets the guidelines for permanence and durability of the Committee on
Production Guidelines for Book Longevity of the Council on Library Resources. ∞

As ever (and ever)
for Renée

* viz., Larkin's "Here" — for "narrative" technique.

CONTENTS

6½ pp.

[wonderful puns; this is a really fine reverie-nostalgia poem, risking the sentimental constantly but surmounting it].

only a lyric, scarcely a thought until last clause; but so focussed because of impeccably sure-footed rhythm, like stepping-stones over a brook...

THE GARDEN BEYOND

36 pp.

One of his masterpieces of soliloquy:
(I've addressed Sargent (Mulcifer))

also this is *the* "feminist" statement
that, I think, must not have
ever been written (certainly not in poetry!)
before — or since.

Also: → See my "note" at close of *poem*, a further
closure (a denouement perhaps?).

A SUM OF DESTRUCTIONS

A Sum of Destructions

Chirruped sparrows,
tipping dawn's top spires,
hurtle out a bell-bright city
in their intelligent wings . . .

last night's squall
drawn off, remote and muffled
waters riding solitudinous
rocks, still mutters

in the hidden parts,
ebbing, beating, of the brain
like some name reverberant
from a forgotten story . . .

light moves, the whole
massed flotilla of morning,
till the hungers, the hatreds
seem fabulous. The sun,

one lot after another,
oversees these various chores:
somewhere a child in a cage,
bodies making a passable

road, a girl passionate
with pain, an old man watching
the world retreat like his
once seemingly endless

strengths. One fills
with awe—as the streets
with light, sparrows brimming
wires, broken windows—

that the earth like some
enduring breath, a song never
balked, should include all,
must be a terrible good.

FRACTIONS

And the pear trees
deep in their white
and the cherry steep
as though climbing,

a luxuriant blank,
a table spread
for fruits to come,
        and I—
moment by run-on moment
the petals fattening—
keep to this book,

assured its black
and white outwit
every trick of color.

But now as I look
out through the dark,
driving rain
        at the trees,
drenched yet glistening,
doubt drums in me

as if to say,
How prodigal you are,
and at your age!

And I feel the rage
of their precariousness,
their swift,
        yet slow-
seeming come of white
and pink,
        and their
even swifter go, they
precious, unique, casual.

Like the lives carrying
on—in the rain a troubled
glow—at bed and board,
at funeral.

What's this old woman like?
A poem, say, by Sappho: glamour
once, sung out of perfect grammar,
now she's scattered pieces.

Well, for all the famines
prosperous in her, the earthquakes
she's supplied the epicenter of
(a captive, ransomed twice,

else sold into slavery
in the Sumatra of her nature,
was she, one market day, despite
her beauty, not abandoned

haglike on the auction
block?), it's no surprise that she,
stripped to if's, but's, or's—
jagged the breaks between—

makes little sense. Pains-
takingly I fill in words, tenses,
seek a syntax that will order them.
What a feckless exercise!

Let those leftovers settle
as they like. After such a life
why spend their lie-about time
straining to remember?

Wrapped by frozen snow,
rains at last renewing them,
the sun will sharpen its luster
on those snippets.

Abruptly then
a shimmer of meaning takes the eye,
the dialect hid behind the verses
Sappho sighed to one especial,
gifted girl.
There, slinking
through in see-through draperies
and glittering rings, its obbligato
wauling cats, the moon plinks
out heavenly undertones.

A friend has found his answer
in a little Italian church;
a sign next to a painting said,
"No writing on this wall."

For all the scribblings already
there, how add to it?
                                "That's
just like me," he sighed.
"Blotched as I am with graffiti,
a bedlam all my own, I have
no room for this latest scrawl."

I doubt that elder wrongs,
however jammed, refuse asylum
to their needier offspring.

Indeed that wall, its martyrs
many times done in all over—
enough to shove the devil
out,
            then smuggle him back
in—admits less, so more,
of its initial vision
than it could do alone.

Belated as he was, how
should my friend have known
he's here to demonstrate
such basic truth?
                        To wit,
refusing to see his mother
in her dying days has served
to clarify—if not complete—
that fresco on the wall.

High-windowed as this office is,
motes bounce about like scrambled sums.
Perhaps it's chaos breaking loose:
in all its skittering, dark matter;
fractals thrummed off superstrings
Pythagoras set going with a twang.
Or remnants of the formulae
a famous mathematician (could
it have been Mandelbrot himself,
rapt in this very room?), scrawled
on the air before him, pondered,
then, shaking his head, rubbed out.

Pythagoras and Mandelbrot,
dark matter, fractals, superstrings!
Much I've to do, bemuddled by
scraps overheard, with such a flock
atwitter in their Institute!

Wryly the overseer in me sighs:

"Why be depressed? You also scribble
across imaginary blackboards.
Figures, letters, parts of speech,
your verses, terse as well as looped,
all would sound out—as they'd compute
into one sum—the universe.

At numbers awkward from the first,
you put your trust in other matters.
Then, to cap it, you missed out
on fractions."
                    I'd forgotten that.
Was it a week sick in bed?
                    "Or did
you scamper off inside some book
whisking you years and worlds away?"

Maybe, as rain, pocking the window,
whispered syllables I almost
understood, I looked to the company
of clouds, those that seemed to peek
into the classroom at Rosie,
some mysterious sun snagged wild,
a blaze, among her lustrous braids.
To deepen them, brand them my own,
I dipped their tips into my inkwell.

"A blaze indeed. But not the kind
you fancify out of the trifles
you recall.
          Real choking smoke—
your baby sister's wail arousing
you—surged from that snowy midnight
fire scouring the rooms
above your father's store."
                         We, clinging
to each other, breath a rasp
of smoke and frost, groped through a window
out upon the store's tin roof
and cowered there—
                    "your neighbors hid
behind drawn blinds"—
                       until the town's
one fire-engine came with ladders.

Before the dawn, concerned about
my closest pals, the Rover Boys,
the Merriwell Brothers, cheek by jowl
with Huckleberry Finn, flouting
orders—
         "any instant ceilings
might collapse"—
                  I sneaked upstairs.
Surely they, as smart as plucky,
must survive?
              "A combustible lot,
like the svelte manikins your father
loved, dressing and undressed,

to dance among, scorched they'd been
and soaked beyond recovery."

Penniless, my parents left
to try another spot, while I
in hand-me-downs—
                    "bestowed on you
by neighbors glad to help you out
of town"—
                    moved in with my grandparents.

Weeks at a time, my grandfather
away, lugging bulgy satchels
along miles of mills, down aisles
on aisles of women stitching, Bubi
and I lived in a private world,
the loving one inside the Yiddish
that she taught me.
                    "Whinnying
from out her stories, Tartar horses
clattered among her kosher dishes,
quaking on the shelves."
                              Yet somehow
never shattered.
                    Leaped from sleepy
pages, feathers bristling above
the shouting, booted horsemen, up
in arms to greet them, Hiawatha.

"Still that Yiddish mutters on
there just beneath the skin of English
you strut round in,"
                    like my father's
cast-off, baggy clothes?
                              "Father
nothing. Rather snitched from glitter-
some godfathers who, had they
heard you—at best, like Proust, a Jew
de mots, at worst a gallimaufry,
your father's huckster, many-broken

lingos squawking through your speech—
could not have held back snickering,
'Oy Oy Oy that Shakespeherian Rag!'

Mongrel tongue that Yiddish is"—
any more than hybrid English,
dressed to kill in pilfered silks
and scents, in words, more fragrant?—
"aren't you afraid one day,
resenting your rebuff, it yipes
'Auf de gonif brent de hütel'?"*

Nonsense! You must know I revel
in the piping hot through Yiddish
of the desert winds and spices,
adding savors to my English,
sparkling glances, bodies twined
in twirling dances.
                     Intimacies
too, however terror-bred
by Cossack raids one burning night.

"As on that icy sunset sparking
off your moony specks, your school
let out, you darting along alleys.
There, hard on your heels,"
                              the Polish
kids! their rocks sped on by "Yid!
Yid! Yid!", attacking,
                        "bring
your Bubi's nightmares up to date,
those intimacies terror-bright
you revel in!
              They, like your books,
about as potent as your shouting,
breathless, from your house's stoop:
'You better watch out: I'll get my father's
Hungarian Fits!' "

* "On the thief the hat is burning"—
telltale sign of a guilty conscience.

13

                    For one a born
yeshiva bucher, much more grim
than any such attack, on school's
first day the grumpy principal,
discovering that I, who'd romped
through Scott—
            "and snooped around in Have-
lock Ellis too!"—
            had not yet studied
fractions, put me back a class—
a wound deep-down not likely to heal.

"To make so much of one small scratch!"

Such childish hurt is, for a child,
a hurt enough.
            "Was it not cauterized
by fires flared out everywhere?
Flared as they did around your kin,
packed off to witch-kept oven-flames
your people fed.
                    See! See!
Their ghosts swarming in a cindered
cloud, the nightmare rides you, rides"—
whose hat is that, whose eyes, glinting?—
"through the middle of their rout.

There, glared at you, the hat
burning on your head"—
                    Mother!
How could you have joined them?
You belong to another world,
another time.
            "Storm troopers rampant
in her mind, she, taking things
in her own hands, eluded them,
her ashes scattered to the seven
smoke-thick winds."
                    She strides ahead
as if to catch up with my father
on the spunky horse that, bucking

14

like a Cossack prancer, tossed
him to that distant, other side.

"And do you think your flighty poems
will keep you high and dry? Prepare
them carefully as you like, how far,
even sped on by some later reader's
sighing, can they hope to fly?

Well, wherever they happen to land,
one thing is sure: you'll never catch up,
a link, those fractions, ever missing.
Being missed, significant
as any word, slight by itself,
its sentence hangs on for dear life.

Not so different from the English
your Bubi"
                —loaded down with family,
her nights peddled away at blouses
piled on blouses—
                         "never found time
to learn."
                Yet through the days on days—
"days often turned into a churning
midnight sea heaved over her"—
she kept a kettle whistling.

And kneaded dough, suffusing dawn,
our waking house, with cinnamon
and almond.
                Candlesticks she polished,
the samovar her great-grandfather
rattled tall tales from, till hoary
faces beamed, wild festive times,
"the company she kept wherever
she might be."
                So haven't trifles
you dismissed—for most of us
more relevant than fractals, super-
strings—made up the loss a little?

Trifles I, confusion settling
in, can cling to still, as to
that pack of clouds, a maple rippling
below, serene within its plumage.
Like those braids which haul me out
of places darker than they, one blink
a blaze, the next a halo winking,

while out of her broken Polish
past, hardship heaped on hardship,
Bubi, shuffling cards between us,
keeping pace with blizzard evenings,
once more teaches me that in her
I've a place to stay, she tidying
up, serving cups of hot tea,
"yes, with lemon."

My belief that in this poem I'd found
a place abidingly bucolic proved
increasingly ironic.
                        Soon enough
I saw it was at best a place to visit,
not so different
                    from Nazareth,
Bath, East Greenville, sleepy hamlets
of my childhood:
                    good for musing
rambles, good also for being confused
by subtle changes
                    as by features
earlier incomprehensible. Hamlets too
like people,
                    quaintly charming
or brackish for waste, the industries
that failed.
            Out of this friend
arbors sprang up, meadows surrounding,
fluting birds;
                    then real estate
took over, built condominia and malls,
become an instant slum.
                            A few,
dim-lit, raucous taverns I now & then
drop in on,
                    confide in me what
developments have come along, tidbits
of local scandal.
                    Rowdy tales
they tell of former times intrigue me
even more,
                    like certain houses
in my hometown I overheard mysterious
whispers from,

                    goings on behind
drawn blinds which furnished forth my
dreams.

        Ironic that I, still
amazed by these, still search in them
for the bucolic, primal scene.

I

Why should it ever be satisfied,
the mind? Changing every instant
as the instant changes, it knows
without knowing only by going
it remains.
             So this wave on wave
erasing each other, ruffled shift
cast off, another and another
for the body twisting
                         underneath,
but never caught. Even sitting
still (every leaf fluttered along
by the wind, the birds swept
past their flight)
                   careers us on.
However many thoughts we entertain,
not all together can account
for the world or the rootedness
of this yearning to be satisfied.

II

And so, to accommodate our sense
of things—a woman lightly touching
up her mouth, the sun entirely
engaged,
          a nearby brook absorbed
in the assorted scenes flashing by,
the swaying sedges hedging it
like the flowered skirt the woman
twirls around—
                we, recognizing
one mind scarcely enough, profess
to be of several, body straining
also to participate.

And then,
for a single, blinkless beholding,
we are—but not the mind, never
the mind, O never, as it crouches
like a savage ravening in his cave—
satisfied.

The nettling heat huffed
against you trying to nap, a voice
you long ago forgot, commanding
and yet dulcet too, pipes up.

And once more, securely wedged
between grandparents in the battered
Apperson, its cut-glass vases
and its lacy curtains gone,
you're on a soggy August evening
drive. Your father, spurs and all,
hunched over this mettlesome bronco,
bridling at his sense of wrongs,
your mother sways from side to side.

The meadows with their heady scents
waft by, the mountains, undulant
as music, while the voices, murmur-
ous, and underscored by chirrings
like first crickets of the car,
swarm over you.
                    "Poor homely Frieda!
Few enough the choices she had.
Still to have to settle for
that Hermann the Furrier!"
                            And he—
cane punctuating his walk—stumps,
panting, runty after Frieda the Big,
her flushed, begoggled face puffed up
as with a locked-in scream.
                    What did
father mean "He's too much for her?"
His wooden leg?
                    The barns, past dusk
their ruddiness still deepening,
the silos, crammed with summer, loom-

ing over the spacious land, the creaky
covered bridges, and the splinter-
steepled churches multiply
their shadows.
            These, as if enamored
of the voices, cluster round;
for the lidding dark (the dramas
mid-career inside) the fragrance
steepens so that, like a bee
crept into a larkspur, closing
as a night-breeze fans, you drift
in semi-drowse.
                    "Something's got
to be done about that tsatske Edna."

"Cheap, painted shiksa, throwing
our Ben's hard-earned money away
on stuff that barely covers her."

Striding, tall, willowy, sleek,
in her short skirts the shining hub
of his heartbeat, is she not worth
his every cent? Who'd not be gladly
spent on her?
                Why reveries ago
you reeled her in to your expanding
gallery.
            Now she flanks buxom
Susan in your father's dry-
goods store, wobbly high up on
a ladder, you its happy prop,
cheek by cheek with Vilma Banky
in a diaphanous negligee, fleeing
the villain on his palatial yacht
by diving into the sea:
                            O how
she bobs upon the breakers, throbs
upon your breath.
                    And as you thumb
these snapshots that the dark develops,
the future surges through your limbs
sprawled out.

　　　　　　　Suddenly the car
sputters. Your drowse wakes to night-
mare: father has forgot to check
the gas again!
　　　　　　　The car stalls.
At once he shoves the back door open.
"Well, son, it's your turn now."
And you, feet dragging, must step
out—the dank air, rushed to greet
you, hard to breathe—into the vast,
uncharted dark.

THE ARGUMENT

This thing we've had
between us almost fifty years,
thin it is, like the skin
on a drowsing sea.
        And yet
in this bewildered world it has
supplied a shelter. Looks
your eyes
        beamed forth
in all their openness first
welcomed me, wreathed in green
cool shade
        a garden makes
shedding bounties on the earth,
the tropical, small breezes
in your breath
        remitting
fragrance out of flowery trees.
Years past, though we cling
to that skin-
        thin thing
like the caul of a dreaming
wind, almost anything can break
through,
        the wind itself
awakened into flinty blasts.
And yet like edelweiss perched
on a precipice,
        a pansy
just below a lichened, tottery
boulder, as long as it lasts
we are in out of the cold.

THE MOTHS

(remembering Howard Nemerov)

This is a poem about a poet
moved by a like-minded naturalist,
memorable about the ephemeral,
to compose a wistful poem,
both of them in turn
                    moving
me to insist—even as I take off
from the naturalist's observation
"In the world there is nothing
to explain the world"
                    ("except,"
I mutter, "the world, the world")—
the moths, momentary in that poem,
clinging to a sun-warmed, winter
wall, momentous enough:
                    a flake-
like drove which, even as, packed
in its skin, it sounds out self-
hood, highlights the opaque,
brooding dark.
            These copulars
in their incessant bouts need each
other, one the winner at one time,
the other at another, till dark
itself goes out.

A corrosive odor
staining through which she
and only she can know, she holds
herself at arm's length.

But wrangling galore
gangs up again in languages
so alien a civil war breaks out,
the devastation rage begot.

Rages at some one
trivial rejection, some neglect
she had outwardly forgot,
on which her ages,

ever working, built.
Morning and an early spring
rehearsing their assorted airs
might help.
                    But there,
like a thing nightmare gave
birth to, an owl-eyed neighbor
boy who beats his tricycle,

roars at its wheels
to carry him across the desert
to his family and the rest
that they consider him—

his nature natural—akin
and to sound the joys he yearns
for in himself. But times
and places, bobbing

everywhere at once,
confound him; and the faces too,

each face a mob of taunts.
How make an any one

from shifty mother:
wife: daughter: also sister:
often a stranger, dust so close
inside the laughter?

A CRUST

Hordes of mouths groaning
in you, mouths ground in mouths,
and you here alone to feed them,
did they finally, despite your
many wily ruses, devour you?

Years later I hold out
these crumbs of breath, not
to feed you or to bring you back
to those interminable gnawings
hungered the more they ate,

but to say I understand
far more than I then could,
when you, to my irate rebuking
you for sloth, deception, worse,
wistfully replied, "Why, Ted,

I have many generations
of runners to rest for." Avid,
breathless, naked men, each one
passing the torch to the next,
each, past death, going on:

their ragged, famished
ghosts seem to bite at air.
It is my hope that you, rather
than joining them, sit somewhere
in easy, well-fed amusement.

It was a side of you
that had to starve, talented
though you were for it, betrayal
requiring you gnaw on yourself,
as though you were another.

Such the crust I nibble at.

I

A different tongue, you think,
would set you free. Imagine songs
you, disabused of old entanglements,
might sing. But only out of mastery;
you must belong to one another.

Still it may be ignorance enjoys
advantages as well, a freedom
all its own.
            Early on, innocent
of French, were you not charmed by
Mallarmé, his cadence, sly as silken
clouds, an incense, high above
the daily stench?
            You, better
off than those inhabitants baffled
by knowledge, furled out yet another
veil upon those veils on veils
that Mallarmé disposed.
            So you
were happy, your first carefree days
on the rue de Fleurus, translating
Baudelaire at sight.

II

            And yet a little
learning can take you a long way,
the way your good friends felt
living in Rome:
            as if, they come
a great distance, this world, going
on for centuries, had all that time—
hoarding spoils, the masterpieces
tumultuously displayed, one street
skipped across to another epoch—
been rehearsing just for them.

Hoarded as well the masterpieces
of savage agonies, slow griefs,
crustacean-like carving nacreous
shells meant to be held up to
the ear.
        Even particles swept by
from countless tombs, what else
but traces racing on, a multitude,
of golden, winged feet—the lasting,
momentary heroes, monsters, gods.

Especially in the moonlight,
ruins again spruced up, identical
with their makers' fondest dreams,
their residents exultantly in place.

III

And yet, a short time passing,
this town is not exactly paradise,
not exactly a triumph in which,
from Cleopatra to the latest cats,
the whole glorious story floats by
and every day for your amusement.

Every day you stumble into things
intransigent. Acts too, that look,
that voluble body Italian,
so emphatic with its tangled
sentiments it proves impossible
to comprehend.
                May it not be,
congested in the least syllable
of words you thought you understood,
a rush of sibyls, furies jarring?

IV

Step outside. Incessant screech:
the Vespas sputtering, tour buses—
gas fumes mixed with cat and human
piss, confused with dust swirled up
from charging chariots—plunge by
as though they dash through you.

Even rain insists on spitting
out its brusque argot, while snow
flurries like glances from a statue,
stony vision sylphs bestow.
Its aqueducts become the Maxima
Cloaca, the Tiber shows you here
a scummy froth, there a moldering
debris, you wiped out by grimacing
faces piled on faces.
                    And still
you're not neglected: beggars first,
pickpockets too, fast after them
in packs the crow-black priests,
regarding you superior to local
flocks for fleecing, scurry round.

V

So times arrive when you indeed
feel free, maniacally free
of everything, including yourself.

At least the first estrangement
was your own, one you could feel
at home with not being at home,
the world solidly against you.
Its tongue, often betraying you,
still filled your mouth with honey.

VI

In the night the city shifting
its river, railroads, avenues,
the churches, squares, and fountains
seen in a different, glaring light,

you lurched among its shady slums,
its reeking butcheries, uproarious,
mobbed centuries on the loose,
how will you ever find your way?

As though your most recurrent dream
of straying about in some familiar

now topsy-turvy metropolis—
name the place, the street you've stopped
at, people you have stayed with, loved,
your pockets like your mind stuffed
with big black churning holes—
a dream too wild for sleep alone,
had floundered through your waking day.

VII

A slang sidling by, the tongue's
guises and disguises, con men,
gamblers, dandies, pimps, this grande
dame (a tart?), so artfully veiled,
do they, greeting, deviously
seduce?
          This way such foreign tidings,
much more clearly than your mother
tongue, declare a basic truth:
the terrible tenderness, for aeons
ripening here,
                    through bloody crimes
and ghosts—yourself a ghost just
passing by, lost in the stagnant air—
becomes that peace poured over you
past understanding.

echoing cries rouse up
in me, rigid cries of faces
eyed with fire, so that quakings
rack my body.
               I listen but—
I who had my clever phrases ready
and could, I thought, take any
dictation—make out
                      nothing
past the shoving and the shrieks,
the violent stink, in boxcars
hurtling down my mind.
                   Lost
years dumped, the anonymous scars
and terrors, amount to less
than garbage.
             The tears also,
the tides on tides of them, crust
silt-like in a cellar. Still I,
who thought myself
                  an inn
ensuring easygoing hospitality,
must somehow push on through this
refuse.
          My once cocky words
mean something different, vistas
hid behind the cheerful ones
I framed.
           And I shudder even
as I strain to see, shudder that
at last the scene's about to focus
every bit of moaning.
              Will it
shape into the word I cannot hear
since it requires every scrap
of air,

I meantime no more
than emptiness of hands abandoned,
eyes confounded in their sights,
one of those blind mouths?

One of those who keep
bad times going, you give
them all you have; avid still,
they hang round for more.

Better things may be
happening just next door.
But you are much too occupied
to notice; or if you do

it's mostly to complain
about what they have deprived
you of, you ransacked all
the more like a house

ragtag, brawling troops,
offscourings of a cutthroat
nation, swarm into. Or moving
farther back to a dark

age that submits you
to the ruthless inquisition
hunger manages, the wilfulness—
a tyrant—of your anger.

First a lava bubbling,
it slowly fisted into rock
which you, proud of it, stuck
fast to, will endure

to the bitter end.
Bitter enough on the way,
you clutch its cold around you
against the outside

world. Your fidelity
must impress, relentless

desert years which you sustain
and with scant water

beyond tears, passing
through those barbarian tribes,
envious of their spangles,
orgies, rituals, gods.

Your genes, engraved
more deeply than the decalogue,
tick away—a homemade bomb—
their ancient destiny.

The tribes of Levi,
Judah, Dan composed the wailing
wall you are, the pyramid.
And though they acted

as if you were not there,
they felt you, an uneasiness
of that already stirred in them,
a distress forever stable.

This complaint a classic,
what if it takes turns personal?
So doing, renewing itself,
it remains the same.

WORKING PAPERS

"Here in 1989 he's jumped
back to 1929, its long crisis;
breadlines he once
                    joined
he's jam smack in the middle
of. But mainly
              he curses
out, ready to impeach—'that
lump of suet!'—Hoover."

"So that's what lies in wait!
But anyone with a memory
as blurred as ours
                    is not
likely to make it back so far?"
"Scar tissue,
            the deep-down
gouging of resentment, clamps
inside us longest."
                    "You mean,
heaven help us, we're bound
to end up
          with old Reagan?
Wasn't it bad enough to suffer
him in person?
              Why, beside him
Hoover seemed a statesman
and philosopher!"
                    "Well, maybe
we can order up our future:
Allentown, say,
              a green place
our childhood unfolded in."
"It's hardly my idea
                    of heaven."
"Better than our years in
those dust bowl

43

                    cement-mill
towns, incredible now as Petra.
There once more,
                    the Rose
Gardens may pervade the streets,
the Little Lehigh sparkling."

I see an intentness in you
as of one gazing out a window
to the far distance for something
gathering there, a face perhaps
strange as it's familiar.

At once I sense you too
are watching someone watching
in your head, like mirrors clear-
eyed in a veritable Versailles
of watching.   In turn I peer
through you to the next onlooker,
the next and next until I feel
I've mined them all.   This spot,
small as it is, but one blink
brief, the whole world wings
to through our hands clinging
to each other.   Stars may borrow
light more readily from remotest
kin. And waves lunge far above us,
far beyond, yet, of a single water,
cannot make a sea as uniform
as ours.   And because we've been
so intricately interknitted,
the lines between us drawn out
long yet taut, we're free.

Wherever the waves have ended
and the sun has set, the starlight
fettered in some far-gone time
and place,

                    or in a time
and place not yet named or met,
already I, my hand through yours
outstretched, can spy those faces
blending in your face.

THERE

I

Where does this "there" come
from? That is the question
that intimidates all answers
like looking up in astonishment
to see a rain falling as from
under your eyelids.
                                A man
here, a woman there, hurrying
along, drops' splintered shadows.
A tear-drenched covey of cries.
Cars slithering by with who
knows what daunting ideas
sped inside.
                        At that a lull,
a slow, grey, drizzling space
in which anything can appear,
as easygoing as an amble
down the street,
                                its rumble
of humdrum instruments—rain
and traffic, slouchy, tattered
musicians playing for themselves—
barely making it into your head.

You turn the corner. The rain
stops. And there, where you
and many the times had strolled,
a something blazes out as if
awaiting you:
                        the traffic light
stuck at green, clouds soaring
into spired scapes your ablest
dreams would have to quail before,
the crumbled red-brick buildings
aerial, transparent, daring
time its seamless length.

II

Go ahead, roll around
in your life like old cat Hoppy
in the dirt. Good for ticks,
fleas, itches, an ecstasy
of scratching.
              As that Greek
who knew a thing or two advised,
that's how to come clean.

Then for one second at least
you stand out in the open,
lure to the lightning,
singing lustily,

                    "Here I am! I'm here!"

III

till, the light changing,
rain in flurries starts again,
nothing but cold rain; the sky
for swiftly driven, darksome clouds
as turmoiled as your thoughts,

again they press into the question
you suspect you'll never answer,
never beyond its self-consuming
moment believe it here, there,
anywhere.
              Rain falling as from
under your eyelids, cars slithering
by, mud splashes up against you.

SHORTHAND

The great draughtsman is bound to reveal the utmost . . . in him . . .
in any scrawl whatsoever.
                    —Bernard Berenson

I

With penmanship like yours
the scrawl itself takes off,
a stroll for strolling's sake
that revels in each footstep
as it steps,
            then pauses
at the prospect of a thought
that would explore its private
landscape to the least detail.

Like the wind, steady here
inside our sycamore, as though
beguiled by what it's doing,
by its basses played out through
the multifoliate score.

II

                        Time
gone by, your scribbling settles
into hieroglyphs; and he alone
engrossed in them divines
their sense:
            he sees that you
had found the signature decisive
for the moment, practical
unto itself.
            Yet looking back,
he is amazed by unmapped routes
you had to travel, dead-end alleys,
gullies,
            tedious detours;
mad junkies crouched at every
corner, doorway-darkened sots,
and muggers offhand with a knife.

And were these meant to pay
the mounting toll of the highway
you were after?

III

A shorthand
flourish swept you to your goal.
That scribble, he realizes,
what it did—
its curlicues,
the sure way they go wriggling
down the page—
the treasure,
exciting exactly because it can
not otherwise be read.

There must be, you believe, engraved
inside this stone, memoirs you can read.

A mottled crumb, shot from a peak,
then tumbled round, by wind and water
shaped into a finger-satisfying torso,
tides should still respond in it,
warmth from ancient, careful hands
that may have fondled it.
       And others too:
those voluble leaves ought to relate
their tree's whole ramifying story.

So each drop, plucked from a rain,
should, like a crystal ball, reflect,
not only rain's long past, landscapes
rippled through, but what it's up to:

waking air, rain echoes worlds,
their hoary musics, newforged screams,
here shucked to nicknames you are after,
in the dark brushed—fur tingling—
along your skin.
      Nicknames underscored
by geese inscribing vocables across a cloud-
banked sky, and by a star, remarking mid-
night's depth, as by an Odyssean insect,
marched from one end of the garden
to the other.
      But likeliest, tucked
away inside you, diligent, myriad cells,
each one, had you the ear for it, inspired
rhapsode, warbling forth the pristine,
epic theme.
      Like this stone, nestled
in your palm, now dreaming, may be, back
through leaves, stars, cries crushed in it

to the river of lava, the livid spouting
it once was, its substance nothing
but unbridled speech.
                    How, hunched over—
gist of listening to—itself, should it
do more than thrust a shoulder cold
to everything outside?

I

It's all, you know, a matter
of degree. So a rock's a noun,
a stream's a verb, and inbetween
a tree.
      But if reviewed
that "rock" can be as active
as you like, a thing of wings by
very weight.
      A "stream,"
pommeled by a wintry storm,
transforms into a rigor-mortised
stone.
      And should a tiger,
ravenously clawing just below,
"tree" you out upon a lofty limb,
that "tree,"
            however ser-
viceable to birds, proves an
inbetween of quiverings to rival
yours.
      Or as a blind seer
observed, "It all depends on
how you look at it. Each thing's
a going concern."

II

            Some that
seem a monument time passed by—
you swirled around them like
their flimsy dream—
              if you
could synchronize with these,
you'd spy sweeping along, coat-
tails flying:

       stones are hurled
as much as you, and in their
own good time they plunge
like any cataract
           self-absorbed.
As for midges rushing through
their lives in a single day,
you, could they
           notice you,
would seem a petrified eternity,
as common as the air, shaped
like nothing at all.
        A god
has to be a some body (body?)
who no matter how close he comes
magnificently hides.

A NET

you've long been after
which can snaggle any fish,
any raffish laughter, any wind
however strong its fins.

Like a walk inclusive,
as if sure of where it's going
but enjoying itself too much
to hurry on and not take

in the scene—admiring
the birch, the daisies staking
their own grass-lined design,
the river in its character

devoted to its course—
then blithely rambling as
the road inclines, by ditches,
straddling hedges, fences,

into littered fields.
And gone far beyond, a net
billboards ride in like sails,
tensile enough for highways,

bridges, skyscrapers.
No one notices it—all too
busy doing the things they are,
yet also caught—catching

the noises bubbled out
of a swamp. And there entwined
to braid from them as from
the reeky, luscious mud

new delicate threads,
apparent only in a twilight

which looks heaped upon itself . . .
as on a splendid couple,

for a time so turned
to each other, so turned on,
neither had a moment's thought
to struggle or pull back,

the net, at once taut
and loose for intent looks,
set lightly on their shoulders,
flanks, sweat glistening.

LAUGHTER IN THE DUST

As though one could get drunk
on one's own blood, grown deeper,
richer with time, the seasons mixing
toasts and ices, diverse passions
spicing as they splashed inside
the ruddy must,
               our roses here
in fall break out again, the petals
slack yet flushed.
                  And though that's
where we are, the cool-off going
on, dawn shines, convinced of itself,
wholly occupied with the immediate
changes.
        Yet, as if cracks spread,
spaces are opening in the weather,
like the giant locust that, leveled
by a tornado unexpectedly blowing in,
reveals its elegant, dense rings,
patterning only age and the sedulous
elements can produce.
                     Something kept
in the root-cellar, a long-stacked
vintage wine, pressed from grapes
how many epochs, how many continents,
away?
      And, in this instant ripened—
the lost ones, darkling comrades,
flashing as they bend to drink,
the rains flooding so our roses,
drooping, seem to double blossoming—
that something shoots out windy flags
of fragrance, shoots swift-darting
currents up and down the blood.

Who would have thought—beyond
the muddy wreckage, trees uprooted,
cows adrift—such new delight
could bob from such belated flood.

A PARISIAN AIR

*(after Marcel Duchamp and one of his Ready-mades,
a 50 cc glass ampul,* Air de Paris)

Bought in a Paris
pharmacy, emptied, sealed,
and brought to mid-Manhattan
for emergencies,

this hook-beaked,
one-legged, bird-like bottle
keeps a kind of wine in it,
a lucid outlook,

of good spirits
nonetheless, however shied
about, since aerial. Open it.
A whiff escaping,

slowly, if a thirsty
drinking, breathe it in,
the way a burly summer turns
to light and sweet,

neatly accurate
upon the tongue, inside
each ripened grape: the very
song it, forging,

is inspired by.
So now when breathing,
razor-edged for icy blasts,
draws big, abrasive

tears, at once
this vial will let out
Paris, mild yet sprightly
presence bent to oversee

Luxembourgean strolls,
a feeling that draws paints

to it like greedy pigeons
as they gape to be
so gathered, so arranged
that they are flying, they
are soaring without wings,
are uttered, utterly,

without a tongue, an air
that goes on breathing
long after its original
has turned to other things.

I

This night inviting ambush,
who's to say the local tribe,
like deer among pleached branches,
is not lurking here?
                    The color-
crowded fall, commingled with
the richly crested fowl, recalls
their headdress.
                    A glancing—
more than sinking sun—shoots
from the foliage, of eyes caught
by chanting, fluent as a twilit,
fish-peaked lake.
                    They, centuries
before we came, revered this earth,
its sky and rivers that their diving,
blood-paced, helped enliven.

Seasons winding into dances
would entwine the farthest star,
they informed the breeze with song,
intrinsic to bird dialects.

Campfires flickering under lids,
mustangs loud between one heartbeat
and the next, the shadows quicken,
not out of this rustling, moon-
wicked night alone.

■

                    "For all the wars
scarring this land, the feathers
we had decked us in meant more
than show.

Sprung from out the ambush
of your words, on my prize stallion
I soar among a flight of eagle
arrows, saw-beaked, clawing bird
my tomahawk swooped down.
                              Paints
we dipped from tints exceeding autumn
splashed across the woods: our blood,
soaking this earth, once stained
the teeming rivers.
                    The twilight
of my race come home to roost,
it heaves leaf-thick in the wind,
attuning into winter with our cries."

                    II

For these trees putting on
their usual unusual show, everywhere
proclaiming festival, it's hard
to credit stories he'd have told.

Hard too since there is more
to it than that: at times, although
I'd never lived in Polish villages
with relatives, a sudden Cossack
shouting seems to goad the wind.

A gallop urgent in my blood,
I bear them, having set the mid-
night sky on fire, riding side
by side with whooping Indians.

Still in me must lurk an Isaac
Babel who yearns to be a Cossack,
despite our spectacled bookishness
cantering so that they no longer
watch us in amused contempt.

So I'd emulate a Daniel Boone,
learning this land from Indians,
their animals, confabulating birds,

the joyous wisdom of the seasons,
I, whatever its abiding, all-
exacting terms, part of this earth.

■

Who would think I own a stallion,
lithe and of a chestnut luster,
fitting to the season's usual
unusual show—lovely as it
admits disaster a common-
                              place,
faces taking as they terrify—
a stallion straining hard to join
and lead the thundering herd.

Deep among the loosestrife,
spurred, it gambols to a gusty
laughter in the dust;
                              whenever
it may toss me, it proves faithful.

III

But now out of the moon-lit night
a voice that is the night's begins
(ear cupped, I listen to the sea-
mad pounding of my blood,
                              a ground-
bass swelling from the earth and air
unable to digest the puddled gore,
screams, corpses heaped in pyramids),

out of night, moon-luminous night
that lightens dark to show how much
more dark remains, a voice, compact
of voices, masses chanting, seethes:

■

"Your childhood dread of the devil-
red Indian—a lust as well—his killers

instilled in you, just as they did
of midden us, refracts the darkness
packed away inside your heart.

Can you gainsay that under white,
as under red and black, one blood
and, under that, moon-lustrous bones
and dust inseparate unite us all?

But though we shadow your daylight,
a shadow brighter in the dark,
long you have scorned us, as if
we, less than shades, do not exist.

At last our groans, amassed, forging
one great song, must overwhelm.
Then your blood will rise, strong
as earth and sky, against you, body
one resounding, shattering cry."

IV

But far beyond my childhood scares
and crimes on crimes committed here,
the night made incandescent-darker
by the shadows autumn lengthens,

I recall another lot I'm half
afraid to name—beside their years-
long, global hurricane the Cossacks,
Indians, and Blacks mere local flaws—
lest they like dragon teeth spring up:
Gestapo at my dreams' cross-points
storming away:
                          "How dare the likes
of you assume you can escape
to make it to grey hair, that shaking
hand, a stoop we've not supplied?

Whatever horse may ride through you,
be sure you too end in the ovens.
We, though melted with our victims,

still enjoy dominion savagery,
most potent roused inside the meek,
sustains."

∎

Even so the leaves,
putting on their usual unusual show,
mixed with this sunset's roseate,
prevail.
And as the cicadas begin,
a long-dead friend, over several
continents a fugitive, philosopher
and mentor nonpareil, appears:

"As words have served your wandering,
beleagured people, honor song
and dance, their native land. Sing
as long as you have tongue to waggle;
dance as hard as legs can jiggle.

Sing and dance and sing again,
not to belittle monstrous wrongs,
but to scour the air of those
conspiracies against delight."

The figure turning into mist,
once more the last, redoubtable joy,
a laughter galloping in the dust,
resounds, a nicker that abounds
along the autumn-pungent air.

ENCORE

You're back, old fellow-
traveler, or a fly so like you
I can't tell the difference,
yet more frayed surely

after so many years
of survival, how many miles
of travel, as if you'd boarded
a speeding train you think

(hard as you've worked)
you've winged all by yourself
and managed, staying alive,
to stay on in one spot.

But are you, after that
last encounter with our cat,
really the droopy one that sat
on my page, legs crossed

like a grizzled tailor
threading a specially thin
needle? Your hum, accompanying
chum cricket in the late

skreak of the season,
sounds identical. So too,
like your kindred, you have
flown in here to hunker

down before the winds
or, as images often seem to,
popped from the page to greet
me at the tip of my pen,

leaping to keep up
with my slippery thoughts.

Somewhere, I guess, you'll
find a crevice to hide
in until April
invites you out again.
Meanwhile, have you—up
to jiggling on a pin-head

with other fallen angels—
thread enough to stitch
these seasons together
and the years, the years?

FLYPAPER

(after a drawing by Hokusai)

What's going on here?
It must be a wind we see,
gusty ghost clutching papers
and a body to make out.

Who else but a poet,
ragged gaffer on a spree,
chasing after some fantastic
image of pure ecstasy;

leaped to this sheet,
he's so inspired by what
he draws it sweeps the pages
helterskelter.
                    Higher
& higher they flap, a few
at the top fast popping over,
while specks—are they

letters, rancorous
at being stuck, fly-like
taking off?—every which way
fling themselves about.

Their loftiest,
tethered as to a string,
must be the star he, dangled
from, dare not let go.

He flailing out
such skyscraping capers
which sail him like a kite,
we can appreciate the mighty

transport he's set free
by way of this, his flypaper.

An Old Cart

(on being asked to write a poem thirteen lines or less for an English-Italian anthology)

Thirteen lines? After seventy years
what's left to keep or say?
A few words things are struggling
to shrug off
                    like moldy skins.

An old cart, once crammed with hides
much coveted, creaking—its horse
a jackass after all and crippled—
to a stop.
                    Maybe this way is best,
the space around me growing
and nothing to get in the way
of nothing.

THE GARDEN BEYOND

THE GARDEN BEYOND

(Eve is speaking to the Serpent)

I know that you recoil from both of them.
I know because at times I've had to share
your attitude. That's why I'm here again.
Nevertheless, whatever supervision
you may fear, you needn't swivel round.

These shadows driven over us? Nothing
but late night sifting through first dawn.

This time be sure I've wandered off alone.
He has, if most reluctantly, agreed.
I told him that, to prove myself and, yes,
to prove our love, I'd garden on my own.

Your words, insinuating through my thoughts,
bee-like signaling where nectars are—
and in themselves a nectar tastiest
for their reiterating tang, its sting—
have haled me back for more.
                                    That and this spiky
lilac bush. You twining it, your speech
still seems to spread abroad upon its scent.
As from the laden branches of that Tree.

■

You understand his state? He, his need
strong as it is, must ever cling to me?
Strong it may be. And yet that day not long
ago exposed its ambiguity.
One further reason for my seeking you.

Dawn just arrived, they met, he and his Lord,
as we now do, beside this Tree, perhaps
to benefit from odors It diffused.

And I? As though my birth must wait
on that event, hid in the Tree's
dense shade.
                    For had He not first made
the animals—you too—to try
them out on him as mate?
                              As He
had tried that other one whose tracks,
however long she's gone, go echo-
ing along my dreams. Or is it
merely dust wind stirs?
                              His Inspiration
by, he ran into no difficulties.
None from earliest, disheveled stragglers,
their after-midnight sorties satisfied;
devious pleasures reeking from them still,
each one at once each matted hair proclaimed.

Besides, abounding energy possessed him,
fountaining so we might have looked to it
to crest profusions of newfangled creatures.

But what a task! Assembled in a line
exceeding eye's extent, at this one spot
every beast of the field and every fowl
of the air and after them whatever other
thing can glide or crawl must pause to win
their finishing.

                              ■

                    Carefree, Adam sped.
Enough it was for him to look and listen.
Through each creature's every movement, cry,
its special smell pronounced upon the air,
did not its Maker's eloquence resound,
the name He'd give already one with it?

But then, dawn past, his Inspiration left,
and shortly after, shyer animals
scooting by, his breath began to falter.

∎

Many times before, in circumstances
much less taxing, he, no doubt recalling
other moments with his Inspiration
prodding him, would likewise fade away.

Laboring side by side, we build
a garden crowns the larger garden,
warbled round us from the neighbor
arbors, meadows, brooks. Attuned
those gardens are as to our bodies.

Laboring side by side, a two
in one, until, some thought abrupt
at him, he, starting up, strides
right through my seedlings.
                                        Irate,
I cry out, "Adam!" cry again.
At last he looks around, looks
toward me, looks as though he sees
no one! Or rather sees through me
somebody else?
                        And yet, such impulse
gripping him, the heaven's topmost
sparkling from his eyes, how not
forgive his rapt forgetfulness?

This Eden, my abiding love
for it you know. Still for him
would I not spurn it and, if need
be, overturn?
                    Conceive a garden
can compete with flowers swarming
round me, through me, at his touch.

But then heart wrenched in me: what certainty
must he enjoy, what matchless loveliness,
to draw him off and leave me all alone,
not asked to share?

(could end here...)

■

One dawn, we sweetening
our labors in the garden with our words,
Adam chanced to speak (he never mentioned
it again) of "the time before the Trouble."
When I asked him what that Trouble was—
"A something she had done?"—as if he had
not heard, he, flustering, hurried on:

"Once and long ago, you still
intact in me, this Eden plot
had not yet parted from the rest:
the whole wide world, a garden far
beyond this garden, nestled us,
from dawn to dusk, wherever we
might roam, within His loving gaze.

The flowers, larger, taller, each
a tiny highnoon on its stem,
would nod as if they heeded us
and, buoyant through their lavish scents,
murmured in the loitering breeze.
Then one berry made—of nectar
sweet and lightsome meat—a meal.

The animals? Without a word
we understood each other, loved.
No pruning then, no shepherding.
Our minor duties a delight,
like birds exulting in their wings,
we spent our days in song and dance,
in festive joy admiring."

So charmed was he by what he, saying, saw,
for fear I'd anger him, I asked no farther
what catastrophe destroyed this joy.

With memories as bounteous as his,
and I, despite his much repeated "we"
and "us," no part of them, how balk at his
ignoring me?

■

Oh, yes, several times—
his Inspiration much like him engrossed
by their intent exchange—and I close by,
they noticed me. As much as furnishings,
a floor to scrub, a meal to be prepared!

Else in the open air, I diligent
among my fruits and flowers answering,
their eager scents translation of—worth all—
that complicated talk.
                                    Still I was pleased
and reassured by words I overheard:

    "The reasons for this world, its subtler purpose
    lurked behind? As clear as day and dark,
    the rivers, hills, that Tree. Light the halo-
    ing that focuses whatever is,
    with night parenthesis to keep it all,
    if you but look, the shyest thing, a self-
    declaring word, conjoins the rest to make
    a single sentence. Flowers, birds and beasts,
    My speaking resonant through them, as through
    the garland Eden is, why ask for more?"

Reassured I was, immensely pleased,
to see how much our Lord and I agreed.
So, although His warmth be little meant
for me and even though He'd left, I went
on feeling glimmers of Him in my eyes
and over me, like lying in a sun-
beat field at dusk still mint- and clover-hot.
A music, echoing from every corner
of the sky, reprised by bird and flower,
made my hearing ears innumerable.

■

Such moments he assumed too powerful;
observed firsthand, the least must overwhelm.
Much better retailed in our privacy,
caresses helping me to understand.

And usually that Inspiration would
rush off. New burgeonings and waverings
elsewhere urgent for attention?

■

                              Times
I, in truth, grown restless at such conduct,
longed to follow Him that I at last
might see what stretches far beyond our sweet
yet rigorous confines.
                    "Be content,"
    he says, "like butterfly and bee
    that flit from rose to honeysuckle,
    each a mini-Eden.
                    Don't
    you taste, and instantaneous,
    packed within the apricot,
    erupting from each ripened plum,
    our garden's boundlessness?

    So, lured by curiosity,
    by novel whiffs swirling up
    to their far-off empyrean,
    flocks seraphic
                    often bustle
    here to bask in these the latest
    blossoms of His handiwork,
    but most of all to ponder us.

    As of a twilight God Himself,
    strolling along, enjoys a loll
    within His new creation's spell,
    the uniqueness of our company."

■

Such words to me, he not remembering
that I first stated them, urged when he
stared off, disconsolate, in endless space!

With him by usually—winds from above
collecting like a warbling in the trees,
bird bicker modulated through the swishing
branches—everywhere seems near, seems ours.

But other moments, he prey to some mood,
I strive in vain to reach him. Panic loose
in me, I hear, as through myself, among
the leafy mazes journeys clamoring,
hear from their distant midst loud mockery.

■

Around us the crowded always here and now,
outside does raw air grate upon itself?
A storm, not yet converted into speaking
by His breath that cribs us while it stirs?
Or are there worlds awaiting us and steeped
in pleasures we can scarcely now suspect?

A tantalizing smell as of remote,
mysterious places issues from your mane.
And through your words a something glistens. Realms,
you say, magnificent in ruggedness,
untouched by man or God?
                              Hot on the tails
of geese, flapping strident music
from the sky, that fiery hawk.

Clambering the clouds, then riding,
poised and blazoned, on the air,
see what freedom it enjoys.

Equipped with beak and claws, does it,
swooping out beyond our pine-
clipped closure,
                    live to utter life
thrust wholly upon itself and nothing
inbetween?
                    Or is this garden nothing
less than shadow of the true delight?

■

Those genial messengers—the shining ones
his name for them—whenever they come sweeping
in dumbfound: mellifluous vistas instant
in their voices, from their glances dazzle
of a world surpassing human sense.
The woodlouse, even in its all-engrossing
labors, must it not, jaws gaping, pause?

Often have I marveled at watchfires
strewn, countless, across the firmament
in nightlong vigil or in conference;
their laughter crackles down, one with the breeze,
and ricochets off peaks, trees, our looks,
inside our dreams long after echoing.

So now no less, although his Inspiration
had departed, glimpses flickered still,
chords of that Someone wafting Himself along
on waves of fragrance.

■

                              Meanwhile, Adam strove,
his body clenched, to cope with that parade.

He should be capable of this? Perhaps.

More times than not, however, he is buried
deep inside himself.
                    His "Be content"!
Ignoring me, the riches surrounding us,
content he is to live among his thoughts,
his words and images, as if they make
a world, the world.
                    Outlandish terms devoid
of lasting relish he loves minting. Terms
like reason, scruple, sanctity, which look
to nothing but themselves, content with nothing
but themselves.

■

        Last night when I proposed
our separating, he, dejected, sighed
"absence," "solitude," and "loneliness."
The first time said, yet clearly shadowing
our blessedness.   Small wonder words stick fast
to him like draggled feathers to a bird
that thus forgets its wings intended sky.

Else turning outward, then completely set
upon the complex workings of some dim-
lit galaxy.   Or plunged into his talk's
spring-tide, I joying in it, fretted too,
choking as if, for one such breather, heaping
up fatigue, there were not air enough—

surprised some animals eluded him?

■

One though I am with our garden, wreathing
round me every thing, I saw his stress.
Pity for him, helpless, welled in me.
So too the knowledge eager to be used:
companioning the animals, a part
of them as they of me, I long prepared
for this, learned names murmured secretly
among themselves.   Yet present I am at best
to do—and only when occasion come—
no more than decorate the scene. That
most modestly. "Another blushing rose"
he says, of me once called "the morning's morn!"
Names, it seems, can change as moments do,
as feelings in their fickleness.   Pray tell
why such steadfast will in me, such hunger
swelling for the world at large, a hunger

to be flourishing the fruits amassed
in me, if will must constantly submit?

■

My moment ripe, I, drawing near, whisper,
whisper so he scarcely knows he hears.

Only I was there to recommend—
for time on time I'd watch it, splashing,
wallow forth—"hippopotamus."
A horse besoused must come to this.

Astonishment he's known that I can feel
down to the very roots, like growing plants,
of words, words that hug their things close
as their skins.
                    For him the names—elm, camel,
lark—pop out; then, dragging after, things.
Sometimes he seems to spout more terms than there
are things. Experiments that failed? Or do
such words foreshadow beings on the way,
and feelings too, not yet experienced?
Like his Maker he first says then sees.
Had God not said, "Let there be"?
                                        For me,
speaking garden—individual
each daisy and each lilting comber, neighbor
chickadee that every morning greets
me at my door, a chirrup like a spray
of luscious berries for me in its bill—
each thing comes first, its word then burgeoning,
this lilac from its shrub.
                    So there,
clumping like an earth torn loose,
an obvious, its nose-horn thrust
at us, "rhinoceros."

■

But as his host
of stutterings collects, you slinking by,

he, the first time—barely—seeing me,
in a sudden scowl declares:
                                        "Sin-
        uous as that one is, a stream's
        meander, paused at every turn
        to admire itself within itself,
        perhaps you'd better fix his name."

For you, so separate, superior,
so glossy and aloft with rufous ruff,
voice crested on its hissing syllables,
"Lucifer" I propose.
                        But he, liking
you as much as you incline to him,
"That's much too good for him!" Splutters "serpent."
Then plumps for "snake"; "a spitting kin to sleek
and sneak."
                And, finally, I protesting,
he lours forth "reptile," "viper," "worm."
Apparently no one name covers you!

                        ■

Suspicion in him of our former meetings?
I breathed no word of them. And yet the last
time I returned he stared, brow knit, at me,
sparks out of him I'd never seen before,
a tremor at his mouth that almost said
"Where have you been? What done?"
                                        And standing there
beside him, now peered out beyond the swaying
fields, I felt a strain in him, strangeness
racing through his blood, like some wild creature
scurried through the brush, so crushing out
its rarest pungency.
                        That day, as if
your atmosphere still quivered round, we worked
no more except as we explored the summer
in us to its source:
                        a loving springs,
savage and tender both, past any rapture
till then dared.

■

       Possessed we were
as our celestial guests, the sky-
borne flock that hawk herds into flying.

Shot from us the blinding light
that burst just as the world began,
the burly world and wholly, thundrous,
through our mingled hands.
              That way
we bless us with creation, essence
of beast and bird and flower, bee
completing the deep-throated tulip,
threading the mazy rose.
            Angels
also ranged our stormy breath,
as from our lidded eyes and finger-
tips, swept up past their wings.

Amid our bower's shade, the fire
leaping in us still, choicest
names we give each other. Names
not He can share.
          Why should He think, you too,
we do not know what any tree can tell?
Knowledge it is called, once more the bond,
beyond suppressing bad or good, of bodies
joined.

■

      For that delicious consequence—
the more it promises—I meet you here.
As for the other things you hinted at,
in manner much as word, might take me farther
into being woman.
         But for him a glimpse
of you suffices. And especially then:

    an instant and stake-upright, hover-
    ing, you stood, on me your bulging,
    blinkless gazing set.

                              Next, turning,
with a lightning's flash you dis-
appeared into the grass, no ruffle
there. For him not fast enough.

Had he sniffed, and bristling out of you,
a danger, something basic to himself?

                         ■

The buzzing, mote-like mites attending you
likewise for a moment whizzed round us.
Dismissive of their volubility,
the air's own flitting words, Adam flails
his arms against them, "Pests!"
                              If one listens,
as I to you, their dialects make sense,
a sense of swarming, delicate delights.
These too, His eloquence, a music blessing
us, require blessing of a name.
They crowning you, is it not mimicking
the pride of angels haloed round His head?

                         ■

Proudest I was—
                    why not, I thought,
name each such minim after what
it mainly does, after what
it mainly is—
                    of "fly."

Also, for that so much alive,
a wholly "be," an incensed life,
it needs an "e" be added
to acknowledge it, of "bee."

So too for those your retinue,
as well as their inferior kin,
scuttling things outfitted best
in tiny bits of breath, I hit
on "nit," "gnat," "flea."

                                        Chortling,
        he admitted he'd have settled
        "buzz" and "buzz" on most of them.

                            ■

        Clear it is how much he looks to me,
        he who thinks himself my mentor, lord?
        Less I am to him, for all his lavish
        blandishments, than to the noisy sun
        the moon, shining only when he nods.

        Sees he how greedily the sun drinks up
        life-giving waters moon and earth gush forth?
        And how the moon from out its valleys sheds
        a glow turns earth into a splendid sight:
        moon's feeding bids far different night-things be—
        furtive little families, earth-hugging
        sprouts, more subtle than the daytime blooms.

                            ■

        Yes, these and others, scamperous enough
        to slip among his porous, lazy looks,
        I name:
                    mouse, squirrel, chipmunk, shrew,
                the speed-hid hummingbird, the dark-
                caved bat, the light-enamored newt.

        Thirsting for caresses long familiar
        and familiar, private names, a homely
        concord to their ears, they rush to me,
        bend as for the quintessential Eden
        waters to my deeply mirroring breath.

        Indeed, the females ambling by, lagged
        behind their mates, were naturally my charge,
                the doe, the cow, the sow, the ewe.
        Allowed—like me—but one curt syllable.

■

And my responsibility went on.
Intensified as he slumped more and more.
Sweeping by, for him a less than shadows
the late morning casts, a flock of swifts—
how apt their name burst out upon my lips!
Like comets tipped, they dove into the Tree.

Imagine him among the teeming groves.
Oh he moved through them many times a day,
at my bidding trimming this tree, that.
But however clear each separate voice
replying to the divers probing wind,
tree's name to him as jumbled as its leaves.

Why he can hardly tell the sleekly climbing
from the shaggy low.
                    This towering Tree,
though It declare itself with every breeze.
Mercurial It may be like every passing
second, yet like that wholly Itself.

■

For morning's high-stepped pace,
stooped to as it polishes
each bug, each stalk of grass,
each momentary jeweling dew:

for long-loiterous afternoon,
tracing itself in every twig,
focusing the blinkless light,
His gaze:
                    and for the night,
its richly populated dark,
of deeds teeming as the stars,
there should be time.
                    A time
for every moment meriting
our heed of it, an adulating
name the fitting wreath we give.

■

Like these reports of the supernal breath,
aloe, poppy, tansy, belladonna:
they move earth and sunlight into flights
that know no bounds.
                    Flooded rivers
          I become through them, reflecting
          clustered eyes:
                         an eagle plunging
          out of clouds, first dawn waking
          in its wings:
                    the fervor peaks,
          humped on themselves, in every rock
          must feel as of their primal roaring
          forth, the Voice immense within.

But he would pluck—to his eyes noxious weeds—
many a plant.
                    These, purple-steep, drooping
over with their wealth, are they not lovely?
Not to him bent on his sense of chores.
This too I might admire, emulate,
were it not so fierce against exception.

■

So his raging should I dare to question,
venture hints he ask for some small change.
"Your restlessness will drive us out of here,
this perfect place you take too much for granted!"

Much more than he thinks, our Lord responds
to any reasonable plea. Applauds
it too as bearing out His will. Else why
endow us with such headlong minds, their bounding
goat-like from each crag to beetling crag,
imbue us with the bounty of our senses,
their abounding appetite for change?

Excess he calls it. Yet the zest that I
enjoy, as well as our grateful pride

in what the senses do, the world they show
the wonder of, does that not honor Him,
and gratify?

      So when, this after many
arguments, I managed to persuade him
to request some help among the animals—
I had, no less than he, demanding duties—
God most readily agreed.

             And when,
to make a nipping spice, I blended herbs,
God was—even he must admit—amused.
As He seemed pleased, though Adam frowned,
at my practicality, devising
handier ways to prune the topmost trees.
Had He not made us to attend the garden
and improve it, so to prove ourselves,
He thereby learning more of what could be?

■

And all the animals, it must be said,
by our remarking them hailed from the muck
of the anonymous, at last stand free.
Free to achieve their own identity.

Yet so they stand, alone, remote, opaque,
and isolate, the bond that made us one
with them forever rent? No going back?

May be.
      Why not, once put out, each self-
expressive, not like water slavish to
His ever shifting Face, and not like air
conforming to His ever varied Voice?

I thought you might appreciate such choice!

Nevertheless, this breath from Him, braiding
to us, to them, does it not bind us still?

By stress of such informed acknowledgments,
our searching out with certain names, this Tree,
Its odors branching through our reveries,
has influenced our deepest, hidden thoughts.
As It now floods Its shadow-charming gleams.

■

Dreaming, often I've had intimations
of strange things to come when, for this breath
exerted to its uttermost—yes, His
as well as ours—all the walls are down:

      seasons we have never known,
      yet feel a sudden longing for:
      bracing breezes, jagged ices,
      tempests like the Godly gusto
      at last let loose;
                at other times
      the sun a passion pressing hard
      against our bodies sweltering,
      this land through its luxuriance
      become a glaring, boundless desert.

As we, naming, founded every creature,
it behooves us sound the full extent
of feeling, every mood we're given to.
Why should not nature, in us as in its nature,
try its ultimate resource? Even
if it means going beyond this garden
to the garden beyond, the world that was
before this world, and after too, the rugged
magnificence you've remarked.

■

                        Moments,
      when the dark's most soothing
      and he lies a lovely weight
      against me, a first tremor surges
      through us of the jostling hordes

that soon must occupy the earth,
as in an Eden seed vast forests
spread their shade.
And times also
I, peering, am convinced I see
their faces, hear their jumbled voices,
wave on wave of clutching hands.

Already I miss those masses, windrowed,
sighing like our garden's leafage,
at one wind falling.

∎

Once long ago,
Adam fast asleep in early dawn,
I, restless, slipped out for a walk.
And following a slippery path I had
not known before, I stumbled on a sizzling
ached my ears, yet lured like some new fruit's
ravishing smell.
There, hiding, crouched
behind close-latticing vines, I heard you hiss
a rakish tune swells on and on in me:

Soon heat the hottentot and curd-faced cold
collaborate with slime, ooze,
rot, an oriental potentate
robed as in a gorgeous sunset
(like the plum a harem in himself),
his entourage huge, gorging, iridescent flies.

Hottentot, potentate, harem, what are they?
That teasing trio, slime, ooze, rot?
Did I not see you preen—mane bristling rain-
bows—in a brook, while midges dotingly
whisked round in gusts a penetrating air?

And music hears stampeding inside sleep:
turmoils there are not wings enough

93

to nestle, ears or tongues enough
to feed.

Those captivating, pellmell images
broadcast in me swiftly sprouting seeds.
As did your praise for many worlds-to-be:

> I garden too: sowing, I mean,
> with loving care, to reap a harvest
> Eden never dreamed of,
> wide as the earth is wide
> till now neglected or denied,
> the other, precious, darker side.

The heavens flushing at your song and streaming
ruddy streaks, a stranger world so crackled
in my blood this garden came to nothing
more than dreary routine, dusty chores.

■

Goodly this garden is, yet cramping too.
And mainly of His making, when our own—
the richest working of our thoughts—awaits
to be explored, by use perfected.
                                    Or
are we no more than words God's mouth let loose
to mate with other words, words spawning words,
so spelling out His message passively?

This wisdom you applaud, my character?

I've learned a truth you did not need to teach?
What excess can there be in reaching out
to knowledge that's already swarmed through me,
Him brimful every atom of this world
He's made? And with our help remaking still.

■

That perky hoopoe, perching in the Tree,
a hummingbird, so throbbing it seems still,
the brown-drab sparrows, sparkled in their speech,

94

chirp "Eve! Eve!"
　　　　　　　Even in my dreams
the Tree lights up an ardent dance.
Like moon-adoring stars its figures
twirl round me, while you, a flicker-
ing shade, weave in and out.
　　　　　　　　　　At that
each dancer—is it she who leads
this comely company?—by winds
she's wakened leaf-like whirling off,
disappears inside herself.

　　　　　　　■

Dark flooding in, the final mopping up
was left to me—since Eve is what I'm called,
eve must be my element: to solace
those that thrive, snug only, in the dark.

And yet does not the least, each firefly,
against the night a mighty beam, of itself
lifelong fizzle away to be observed?
Sings and sings to celebrate the bounty,
banquet, of the being given it.
That "look at me!," no doubt Adam would say,
is my concern alone I wish on them.

Our work ended. And the air, roarings,
brayings, cackles, settled to a rustling
waters might express, till, wrapped in night
like petals closing, sleep lapped everyone.

　　　　　　　■

Then it was our Lord, returning, lauded
him, his mastery. Thereat he struts
as if he'd made the world.
　　　　　　　　　　And I, forgot,
rejoin the shade.
　　　　　　　　But I no less forget?
You, concealed in the tall grass, my powers

95

faltering, as He had stood by him,
had stood by me?
     The wind I must have thought,
inspired by its passage through the Tree.
Yet from the start did I not hold you dear,
my one resort?
     As here I am with you.

■

But then I huddled by my husband's side,
both once more nested, an indivisible one.
Or so at least I thought; for he, sighing,
exhausted, if at last complete, fell fast
asleep.
   That is, till I surmised by his
dream's restlessness as by his heavy breath
that he was romping with the animals,
docile to his will.
     And no less romping—
by the telltale feel of him against me
it must be—with her. Sprightly still,
did she not cajole from him her lisp-
thick, languorous name?
     Him with his wistful,
fond remembering of "us" and "ours,"
"we spent our days in song and dance . . . in joy!"

■

This world, what was it like when she was here?
Did it partake of her? How could it not?

 Sometimes the animals—you also—
look at me askance as if
they spy somebody else working
herself out in me.
    Stooping
over a pool, what do I see?
A stranger I almost identify,
telling me by very features
I think my own how other I am.

Jealous? Who's to say I'm not, so bound
by flesh and blood, their argument, the off-
spring of their wrangling and their joy?

So your shrug, coupled with this whisper
sidelong out of you, by what it does
and does not say, has led me to suspect.

Your fear forbids you tell me more? Content
I am to let it lie, to be at home—
so long I've lived in it—in ignorance.
As long as mystery, its gleam, soars through:
dawn's vapors breaking, clearest over me,
my dream still pulsing, her impassioned face.

■

And so it was I murmured no complaint,
while, curled up at my feet, responsive
to its name, not catnip more compelling—
see how wrong you were: naming made ,
the creatures draw away? Far otherwise—
gratefully Puss purred.
                              Sometimes now,
          it's true, mid-speech, Adam, brow
          befurrowed, finds our phrases odd,
          repeats them like some foreign tongue,
          and most of all those I devise,
          then savors them.
                              Else he's astounded—
          blinks, he seeing more than he
          can see—by brilliance of his own
          inventiveness, the world enlarged
          through words.
                              How should he consider
          me, in this as in all things
          a minor part of him—so he
          would like me to believe—someone
          apart?
                  A minor part! Hard as I try,
      I can recall no glimmer of my origin,
      the startling tale he tells.

■

[handwritten: Ha-ha!]

A bloody rib?
Not likely for the rounded shape I've often
studied in our ogling pond. But if
it be, this—and not that rib—the wonder.
Some waking night, I snuggled by his side,
although he clutch me like a something lost,
I, groping, find no scar and nothing missing.

The tale you've dropped sly portions of has glanced
at something different. My own thoughts too,
her murmurings inside my dreams:
                                        scant time
[handwritten: Lilith, first wife.] she had, her patience scant, for God or Adam
both. She being the first helpmate He made
He made a crucial mistake, made Lilith—so
He's said, and Adam also—much too full
of herself.
              Not, like me, full of gaping
[handwritten: Eve's self-doubt.] space to wander in, doubting, seeking.

Impulses sometimes shooting through, impulses
I hardly recognize, do they belong
to her?
          She stubborn, did God cast her out
[handwritten: Very clever Ted!] that she went howling through the wilderness
till she met you? And then what happened to her?
Hardship? Bliss?
                    As ever you, your words
hissed blurring, turn away.

■

                          In distant time
someone may title me—no other creature
fit to keep our bower neat or cater
to his appetites—his "household pet"!
For that, with his dependency so great,
how can he afford to admit to it?

You're right. Far-fetched though his story be,
it pays him to believe it. That way every-
thing I say and do I owe to him.

But his suspecting that I harbor doubts
must fill him with distress?
                                        Leave it at that.
Enough it is he feels uneasiness.
Those two have taught me what I need to know,
they and you, collaboring bedfellows!
And, conspiring in me, she also.

∎

But though he suspect deep questioning
in me, my knowing other than I ought,
still he regards whatever I may say,
the best of it, no more than womanly whim,
at best extension, wayward, of himself.

A name once overheard, its speaker thinks
that he has always known it, has in fact
created it. The fruits one grows, to whom
do they belong but to the land's one lord.

And so spare praise for me.
                                        How can he,
self-bedazzled, recognize a talent
all my own? How, being out of dust,
whereas I—should I accept his word—
am of His breath, his breast, at two removes
from common earth. No wonder I am better
made than he to deal with it, its creatures,
crises, joys.
                    And yet if, like him,
dust I be, dust from which God made
all living things, to culminate in star,
the seraphim, each crammed with life enough
to live beyond itself.
                            The patterning
alone's the difference, the care with which

He, starting with the worm, so learning, then
shaped us.
              First-born Adam may have been,
the medium through whom the heavenly Speech
speaks forth to every thing. But I, He seeing
His work, by trial reforming it, deserve
I not respect?

                        ■

              Midday arraying us,
my thirst, my hunger, at their liveliest,
that Tree seems to reach out beseechingly,
Its fruit so many glances aimed at me.
The bush, its blossoming reverberant,
assures me too of some rare remedy.

Yes, why ...   Yet why desire other than I have?

A cure, your slippery words now intimate,
which, helping me—like you—to shed my skin,
will free the shiny one restive within,
so pry forever his myopic eyes.
As it has opened yours, you seeing me
for what I am, the choice one I should be.
That way it must bind him to me forever,
even as it frees me, free at last
to be, at least, his equal. His if not
those others jealous of their sovereignty.

                        ■

Recoiling from his shadow hovering,
I too prefer the one of me alone?

That Tree, now I look up, aglow as though
a brand-new morning, its beginning and
its never end, were roosting there, the flocks
in dew-wet wings and song reflecting it,
I feel a blessedness.

And so I linger
here alone. Yet listening for voices
that I'd fish from brook and stone.
                     And, yes,
from you. Not least from her who ever goes
before. The secret voice I yearn to hear.

First listen to my own, voice of my will
a steady hum as from that bird-brimmed Tree?
See, the swifts are gorging on the fruit,
its fragrant juices splattered everywhere.

A hum it is, like serried cherubim
within His breath, the syllables of one
tremendous word.
               Yet earlier I could
construe their speech, but now a dazzling trill
is all I hear.
           Should I but heed I must,
the hum grown clear, discover in an instant—
this?—the cure, its one spell-breaking word?
What is it?
         Tell me! Tell!

[Handwritten marginal notes:]

Lilith is equated with Lucifer

splendid closure!

Note: Cd use one last section: Eve, aware of her dependency / Adam's ambiguity, her growing power, his weakening, cd assert both her dependency and superiority by taking care of him more + more as he ages. Lucifer could tell her this, or she herself to prefer it to listening Lucifer who will not respond to it.

✓ The Late Train
✓ A Certain Village
✓ An Everlasting Once 1/2
✓ The Fire at Alexandria 1
✓ House of Fire 3
✓ The Giant Yea 2½
✓ Far Out, Far In 3
✓ After Five Years 2
✓ A Sum of Destructions (2nd vers.) 1

} 2?

80 pp.

[Ruins for These Times   2½]
✓ A Guest   1
✓ The Medium   1½
✓ In This Tower   1

* * *

Caliban Remembers .... 16 } 2?
Every Second Thought 12

* * *   { ***
                  [Recoveries] [40]

The Hook 3
The Storeroom 15
Homecoming 2
The Visit 7
Another and Another and 2
The Present 1   } 3?

1. Recoveries   *\#\#
2. The Garden Beyond [The Garden Beyond] [26]   40
                                                  26
Gunsight ?? (no.)   30